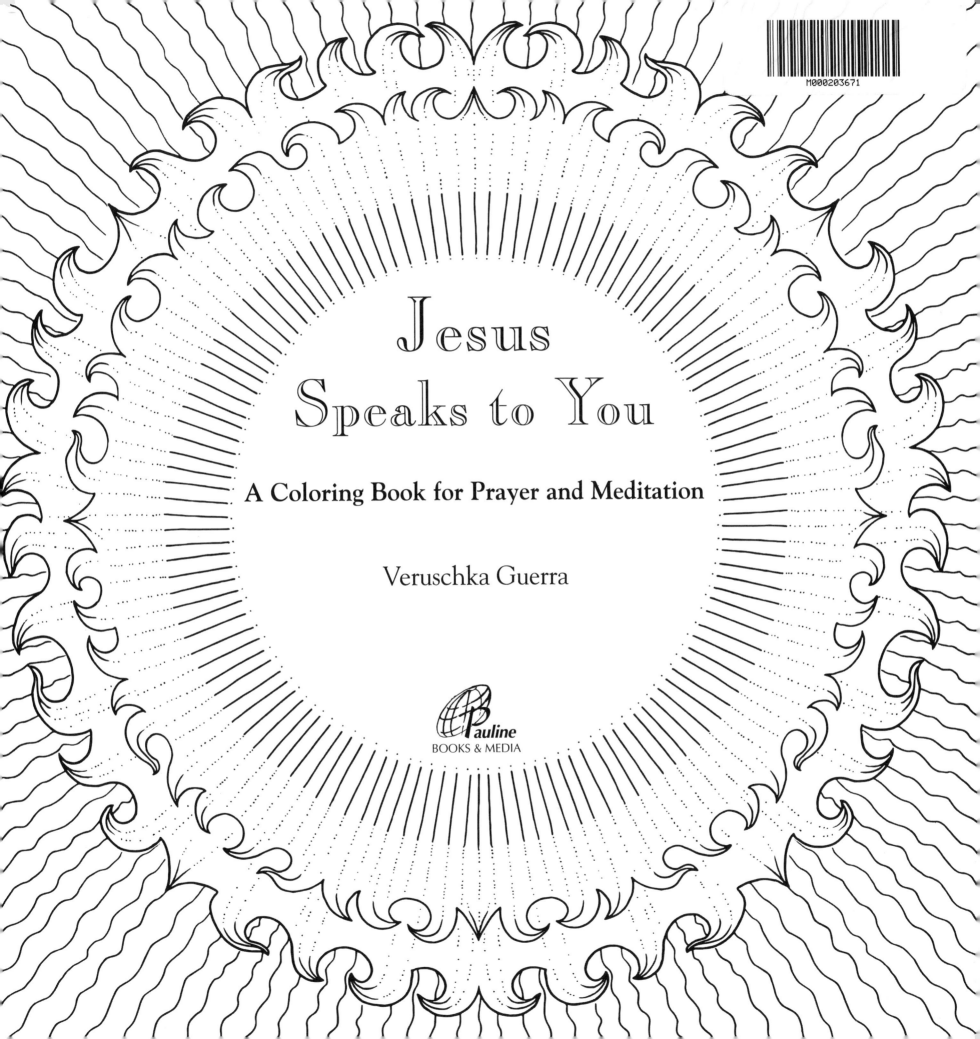

Jesus Speaks to You

A Coloring Book for Prayer and Meditation

Veruschka Guerra

Pauline
BOOKS & MEDIA

ISBN 10: 0-8198-4018-1

ISBN 13: 978-0-8198-4018-9

Book design by Bruno Olivoto

Illustrations and cover art by Veruschka Guerra

Originally published in Portuguese as *Jesus, Mensagens do Filho de Deus em Livro de Colorir* by Editora Santuário, © 2016—Rua Pe. Claro Monteiro, 342, CEP: 12570-000-Aparecida-SP, Brazil

Published by Pauline Books & Media, 50 Saint Paul's Avenue, Boston, MA 02130-3491

Printed in Korea

www.pauline.org

Pauline Books & Media is the publishing house of the Daughters of St. Paul, an international congregation of women religious serving the Church with the communications media.

1 2 3 4 5 6 7 8 9   21 20 19 18 17

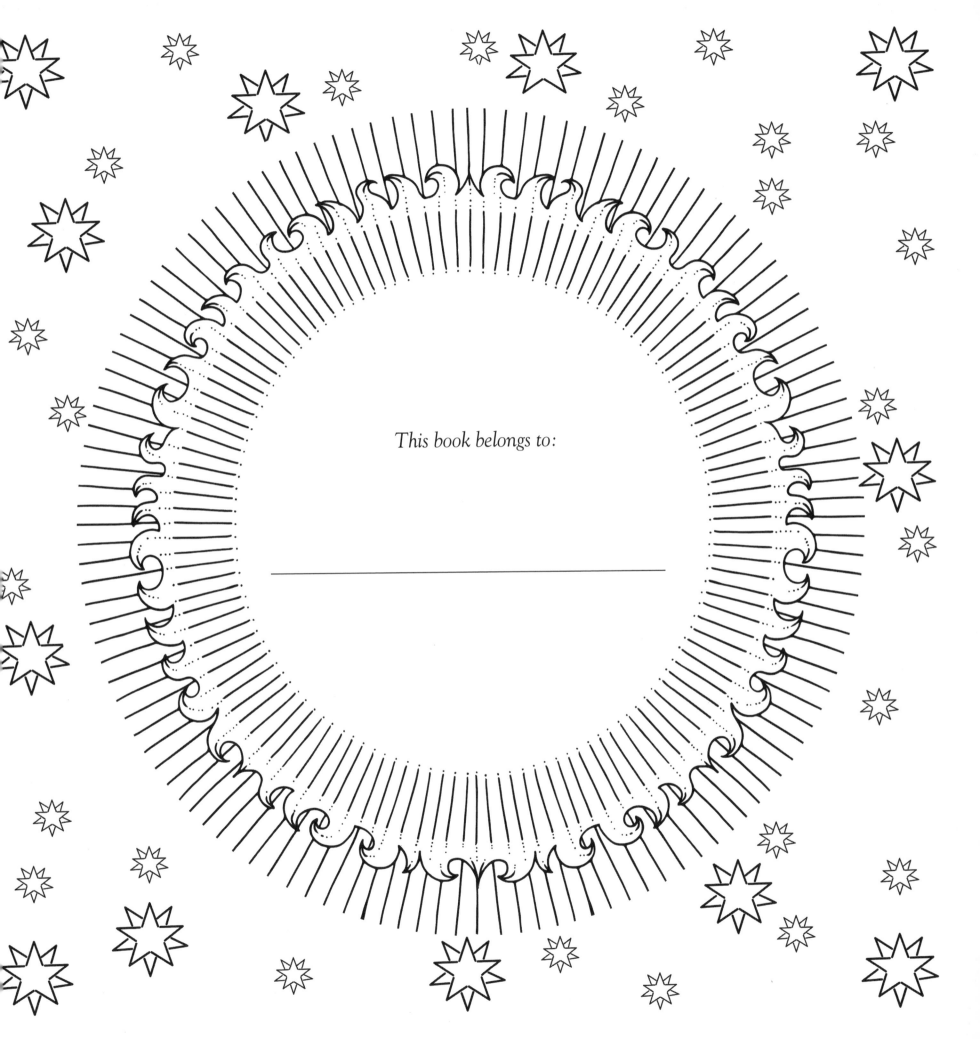

This book belongs to:

_____

Jesus' words and example of
total love have changed the
lives of thousands of people. His words
transcend time and remain alive today
in believing hearts. This coloring
book contains messages from Jesus
to you. His words give each of us
a path to follow, a way of love to live,
and remind us of the heaven
we hope to reach.

Veruschka Guerra

"Our Father, who art in heaven,
hallowed be thy name;
thy kingdom come,
thy will be done
on earth as it is in heaven.
Give us this day our daily bread,
and forgive us our trespasses,
as we forgive those
who trespass against us;
and lead us not into temptation,
but deliver us from evil."

Matthew 6:9–13

The Beatitudes

"Blessed are the poor in spirit, for theirs is the Kingdom of Heaven.

Blessed are those who are mourning, for they shall be comforted.

Blessed are the meek, for they shall inherit the earth.

Blessed are those who hunger and thirst to do God's will, for they shall have their fill.

Blessed are the merciful, for they shall receive mercy.

Blessed are the pure of heart, for they shall see God.

Blessed are the peacemakers, for they shall be called children of God.

Blessed are those persecuted for doing God's will, for theirs is the Kingdom of Heaven.

Blessed are you when they insult you and persecute you and say every sort of evil thing against you because of me; rejoice and be glad, because your reward will be great in Heaven— they persecuted the prophets before you in the same way."

Matthew 5:1–12

"You are the light of the world.
A city cannot be hid,
which is set atop a mountain.
Nor do you light a lamp
and set it beneath a bushel;
you set it on the lampstand, instead,
so it lights everyone in the house.
Let your light so shine before others
that they'll see your good works
and glorify your Father in Heaven."

Matthew 5:14–16

"Love your enemies,
and pray for those who
persecute you,
so that you'll become sons
of your Father in Heaven,
because he causes his sun
to rise on the evil and the
good, and rains on the just
and the unjust."

Matthew 5:44–46

"Amen, amen,
I say to you,
If the grain of wheat that falls
to the ground does not die,
it remains alone,
But if it dies,
it bears much fruit."

John 12:24

"Don't lay up treasures for yourselves on earth,
where moth and rust destroy,
and where thieves break in and steal;
Lay up treasures for yourselves in Heaven,
where neither moth nor rust destroy,
and where thieves neither break in nor steal.
For where your treasure is,
there, too, will your heart be."

Matthew 6:19–21

"Therefore, I tell you,
Don't worry about your
life, what you'll eat
Or about your body, what you'll wear;
Isn't life more than food, and
the body more than clothing?
Take a look at the birds of the sky—
they neither sow nor reap nor
gather into barns, yet your
Heavenly Father feeds them;
aren't you worth more than
they are? But which of you can
add any time to your life
by worrying?"

Matthew 6:25–27

"And why do you worry about clothing? Look how the lilies of the field grow; they neither work nor spin. But I tell you, if God so clothes the grass of the fields, which is here today and thrown into the oven tomorrow, won't he clothe you much better, O you of little faith . . . first seek the Kingdom and the will of God and all those things will be given to you also. So don't go worrying about tomorrow—tomorrow will worry for itself. One day's evil is enough for a day."

Matthew 6:28–34

Matthew 13:31–32

"The Kingdom of Heaven is like a grain of mustard seed, which a man took and sowed in his field. Although it's the smallest of seeds, when it's fully grown it's the biggest of garden plants and becomes a tree, so that the birds of the air come and nest in its branches."

"Go into
the whole world
and proclaim
the good news
to all creation."

Mark 16:15

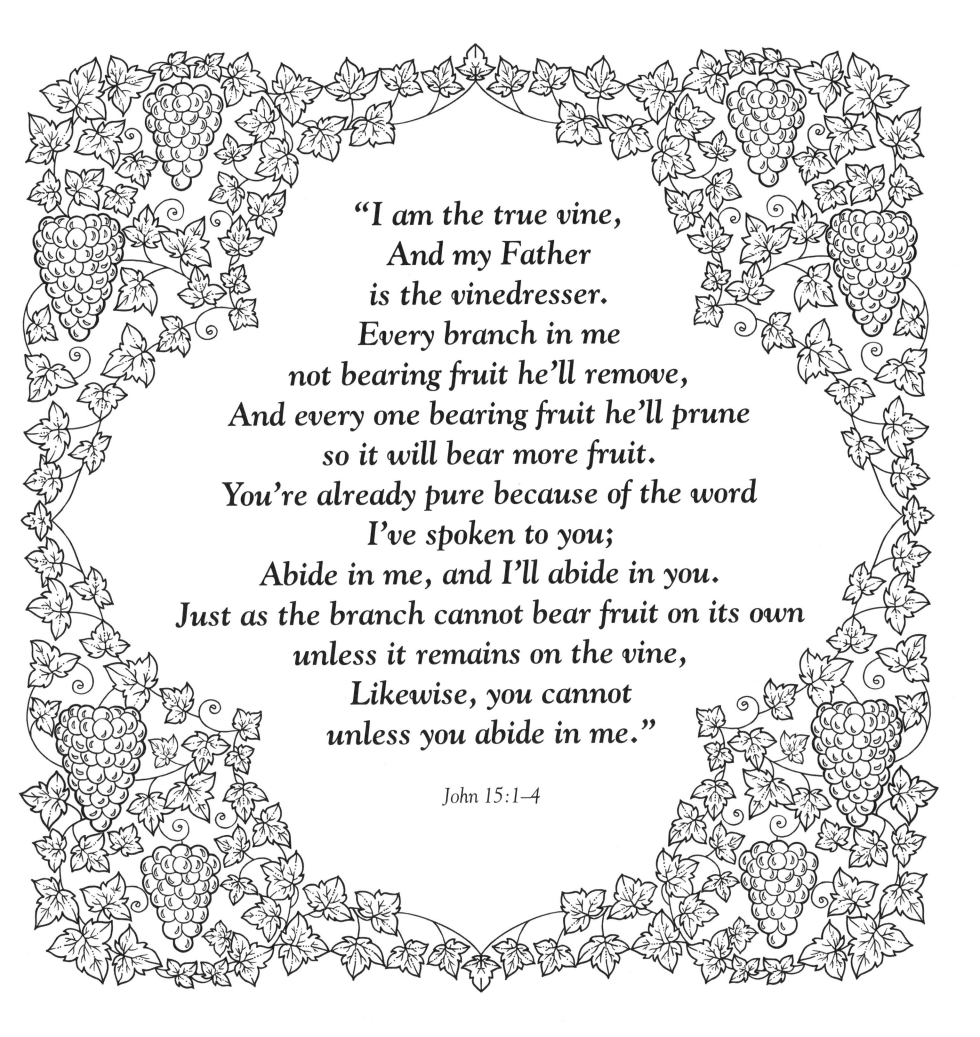

"I am the true vine,
And my Father
is the vinedresser.
Every branch in me
not bearing fruit he'll remove,
And every one bearing fruit he'll prune
so it will bear more fruit.
You're already pure because of the word
I've spoken to you;
Abide in me, and I'll abide in you.
Just as the branch cannot bear fruit on its own
unless it remains on the vine,
Likewise, you cannot
unless you abide in me."

John 15:1–4

The Vine and the Branches

"I am the vine, you are the branches.
Whoever abides in me, and I in him,
he it is who bears much fruit,
For apart from me you can do nothing.
Unless someone abides in me
he's thrown out
like a branch and withers,
And they gather them
and throw them into the fire
and they're burned.
If you abide in me,
and my words abide in you,
Ask whatever you wish
and it will happen for you.
In this is my Father glorified,
That you bear much fruit
and become my disciples."

John 15:5–8

"Just as the Father has loved me,
I, too, have loved you;
Abide in my love.
If you keep my commandments
you'll abide in my love,
Just as I've kept my Father's
commandments and I abide in him.
I've told you these things
so that my joy may be in you
and your joy may be complete.
This is my commandment,
that you love one another
as I have loved you."

John 15:9–12

"Love one another as I have loved you."

John 15:12

The following pages are designed so that after you color them,
you may cut on the dotted line and give loved ones the gift of Christ's message.

"Come to me,
all you grown weary and burdened,
and I will refresh you.
Take my yoke upon you
and learn from me,
For I am gentle and humble hearted,
and you will find rest for your souls;
For my yoke is easy,
and my burden light."

Matthew 11:28–30

"If you love me,
you'll keep my commandments,
And I'll ask the Father
and he'll give you
another Intercessor
to be with you forever,
The Spirit of truth,
whom the world cannot accept
because it doesn't see or know him.
You'll know him,
because he'll remain with you
and be in you.
I won't leave you orphaned—
I'll come to you."

John 14:15–18

"I am the resurrection
and the life!
Whoever believes in me,
even if he should die,
will live,
And everyone who lives
and believes in me
shall never die!
Do you believe this?"

John 11:25–26

"Put out to the deep and lower your nets for a catch."

Luke 5:4

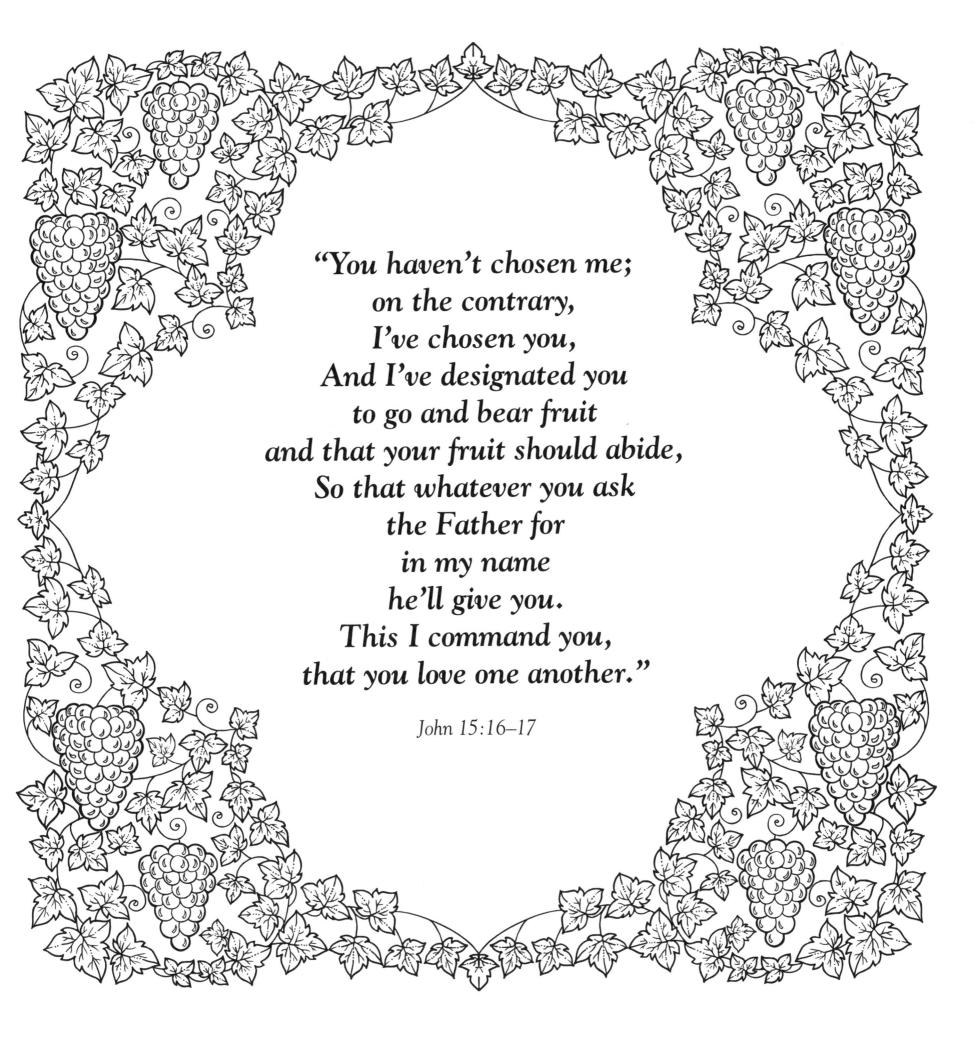

"You haven't chosen me;
on the contrary,
I've chosen you,
And I've designated you
to go and bear fruit
and that your fruit should abide,
So that whatever you ask
the Father for
in my name
he'll give you.
This I command you,
that you love one another."

John 15:16–17

"I am the bread of life;
Whoever comes to me
shall not hunger,
And whoever
believes in me
shall never thirst."

John 6:35